Orsamus Holmes Marshall

The Niagara Frontier

Embracing Sketches of its early History, and Indian, French and English

local names

Orsamus Holmes Marshall

The Niagara Frontier
Embracing Sketches of its early History, and Indian, French and English local names

ISBN/EAN: 9783337147631

Printed in Europe, USA, Canada, Australia, Japan

Cover: Foto ©ninafisch / pixelio.de

More available books at **www.hansebooks.com**

THE

NIAGARA FRONTIER:

EMBRACING

SKETCHES OF ITS EARLY HISTORY,

AND

Indian, French and English Local Names.

READ BEFORE THE BUFFALO HISTORICAL CLUB,

FEBRUARY 27TH, 1865.

BY ORSAMUS H. MARSHALL.

PRINTED FOR PRIVATE CIRCULATION.

JOSEPH WARREN & CO., PRINTERS,

Courier Office. Buffalo.

INTRODUCTION.

THE following sketches were prepared at the request of the Buffalo Historical Society, and read at one of its weekly club meetings held in the month of February last.

They are a humble contribution to our local history, an attempt to rescue from oblivion and illustrate historically, some of the Indian, French and English names which have been applied to the most prominent localities on the Niagara Frontier. The key to the pronunciation of the Seneca names will be found in the Appendix.

BUFFALO, March, 1865.

ERRATA.

Page 6, lines 21 and 22—For "Successfully," read successively.
" 13, line 30—For "Second," read secondary.
" " In the last word, Substitute the common "h" for the last letter.
" 21, line 13—For "Dwellings and Ropewalks," read dwelling and ropewalk.
" 23, line 9—For "Appears," read appear
" " line 28—For "Remained," read remains.
" 28, line 23—For "te deum," read Te Deum.
" 31, line 1—For the asterisk "*," substitute the obelisk †.
" " line 4—For the obelisk "†," substitute the asterisk *.
" 34, In the foot note, for "C. Norton," read C. D. Norton.
" 44, lines 6 and 17—For "Le mer douce," read La mer douce.

JAMES CARTIER, while exploring the Gulf of St. Lawrence in 1535, was informed by the savages living on its borders, that a mighty river, which they called *Hochelaga*, flowed into the sea near by from a vast distance in the interior.* Having discovered its mouth, he explored the stream as far as the site of the present city of Montreal. He inquired of the Indians, whom he met on the way, touching the source of that great river and the country through which it flowed. He was told, that after ascending many leagues among rapids and waterfalls, he would reach a lake, one hundred and fifty leagues long and forty or fifty broad, at the western extremity of which the waters were wholesome and the winters mild; that a river emptied into it from the south which had its source in the country of the Iroquois; that beyond this lake he would find a cataract and portage; then another lake about equal to the former, which they had never explored; and, still further on, a sea, the western shores of which they had never seen, nor had they heard of any one who had. †

This is the earliest historical notice of our great lake region.

Cartier was followed, after a long interval, by French traders, adventurers and missionaries, who, stimulated by love of adventure, the attractions of the fur trade, or

* Lescarbot, p. 300.
† Lescarbot, p. 381.

inspired by religious zeal, were the first to penetrate the Canadian wilderness, and encounter the privations and dangers incident to the exploration of the vast interior of North America.

Before the Pilgrims landed in New England, Champlain had wintered among the savages on the eastern shore of Lake Huron, and had crossed Lake Ontario with an expedition against the Iroquois in the central part of our State.*

As one after another of the principal lakes and rivers of the New World were discovered, they were called in honor of some tutelary saint or patron, some king or noble. The early travelers not only rejected their aboriginal names, but, in many instances, failed even to mention them. The series of lakes on our northern border, were originally considered as but expansions of one continuous river, called by the old geographers Saint Lawrence, in honor of the martyr, on the day of whose festival the noble gulf at its outlet was discovered.

During the three centuries which have elapsed since that event took place, two distinct races have successfully occupied and disappeared from this locality, now in the undisputed possession of a third.

The traveler in the classic regions of the Old World, encounters at every step venerable monuments and crumbling ruins, silent, but eloquent memorials of those who have risen, flourished, and disappeared in the revolutions of time. The Indian, once lord of this New World, now a tenant at the will of the white man, was skilled in none but the rudest arts. He roamed, a child of nature, over the forest and prairie, absorbed in his ceaseless struggle for a precarious subsistence on the

* Voyages de Champlain, Part I. p. 251.

fruits of the chase. He built no monuments and has left no records, from which we may learn the story of his origin, his migrations, his bloody wars and fruitless conquests. The only light which shines upon his annals, is, at best, a dim and shadowy tradition. Scarce a memorial of his former occupancy remains, save the *names* he has bestowed upon the lakes, rivers, and prominent landmarks of the country. The Iroquois dialects still live in their melodious geographical terms, suggesting a sad contrast between their former proud and extensive dominion and their present feeble and reduced condition.

There is no satisfactory evidence of the existence, in this vicinity, of a race preceding the Indians. The " mound-builders," that mysterious people who once spread in countless multitudes over the valleys of the Ohio, the Mississippi, and their tributaries, never, so far as diligent research has been able to discover, dwelt in this locality. The ancient fortifications, tumuli, and artificial structures that abound in Western New York, can all be referred to a later date and a more modern race. But at what precise period and by what particular people they were constructed, are questions which have hitherto eluded the most diligent historical research. The Senecas are equally ignorant on this subject. The venerable Seneca White, a distinguished Iroquois chief residing on the Cattaraugus Reservation, now 81 years old, expressed his curiosity on the subject, in a recent interview with the writer, and desired to know when, why and by whom those structures had been built. Many of them may yet be seen within a few miles of our city, and are certainly objects of historical interest and speculation.

Omitting, therefore, from necessity, any notice of the

race, of whom these remains are the only memorial, we find that the first in this locality, of whom history makes mention, were the *Attiouandaronk*, or Neutral Nation, called *Kahkwas* by the Senecas.* They had their council-fires along the Niagara, but principally on its western side. Their hunting-grounds extended from the Genesee nearly to the eastern shores of Lake Huron, embracing a wide and important territory. In this region, now teeming with Anglo-Saxon life, they reared their rude wigwams, pursued their game, and preserved a rigid and singular neutrality between the fierce tribes that waged their bloody wars on all sides around them. They are first mentioned by Champlain during his winter visit to the Hurons in 1615, before alluded to, but he was unable to visit their territory. According to the early Jesuits, they excelled the Hurons in stature, strength, and symmetry, and wore their dress with a superior grace. They regarded their dead with peculiar veneration. Once in every ten years the survivors of each family gathered the remains of their deceased ancestors from the platforms on which they had been deposited, and buried them in heaps with many superstitious ceremonies. This was called the "feast of the dead." Many of the mounds thus raised may still be seen in this vicinity. A conspicuous one on Tonawanda Island is affirmed by the old Senecas to have had such an origin. The land of the Neutral Nation is described

* It has been assumed by many writers that the Kah-kwas and Eries were identical. This is not so. The latter, according to the most reliable authorities, lived south of the western extremity of Lake Erie until they were destroyed by the Iroquois in 1655. The *Kah-kwas* were exterminated by them as early as 1651. On Coronelli's map, published in 1688, one of the villages of the latter, called "*Kakouagoga, a destroyed nation,*" is located at or near the site of Buffalo.

by the Jesuits as producing an abundance of corn, beans, and other vegetables, their rivers as abounding in fish of endless variety, and their forests as filled with a profusion of game, yielding the richest furs.

The peace which this peculiar people had so long maintained with the Iroquois was destined to be broken. Some jealousies and collisions occurred in 1647, which culminated in open war in 1650. One of the villages of the Neutral Nation, nearest the Senecas and not far from the site of our city, was captured in the autumn of the latter year, and another the ensuing spring.* So well directed and energetic were the blows of the Iroquois, that the total destruction of the Neutral Nation was speedily accomplished. All their old men and children, who were unable to follow their captors, were put to death, but the women were reserved to supply the waste occasioned by the war. The survivors were adopted and absorbed among their conquerors, and, as late as 1669, a small remnant was found by the Jesuit, Father Fremin, living within the limits of the present county of Ontario.

Such were the predecessors of the Senecas. A little more than two centuries has elapsed since they lived and flourished in this locality, and no evidence of their occupancy now exists, save the rude mounds which mark their final resting-places. Scarce a trace of their language remains, and we know only that they spoke a dialect kindred to that of the Senecas. Blotted out from among the nations, they have left one conspicuous and enduring memorial of their existence, in the name of the beautiful and noble river that divides their ancient domain.

---

* Relation des Jesuits, 1651, p. 4.

A long period intervened between the destruction of the Neutral Nation and the permanent occupation of their country by the Senecas. For more than a century, this beautiful region was abandoned to the undisturbed dominion of nature, save when traversed by the warrior on his predatory errand, or the hunter in pursuit of game. A dense and unexplored wilderness extended from the Genesee to the Niagara, with but here and there an interval, where the oak openings let in the sunlight, or the prairie lured the deer and the elk to crop its luxuriant herbage.

The Senecas continued to live east of the Genesee, in their four principal villages, until the year 1687, when the Marquis de Nonville, then Governor of Canada, invaded their country with a powerful army, and, after defeating them near the site of Victor, in Ontario county, drove them from their burning villages and laid waste their territories.* The humbled Senecas, influenced by their superstition, never rebuilt a solitary cabin. Their abandoned homes long bore witness to that most disastrous era in the history of the confederacy. We next find them in scattered villages on the banks of their favorite river,† in the fertile valley of which, they resumed the cultivation of the maize, and recovered, in some degree, their former power and influence.

During the Revolutionary War they espoused the British cause. The atrocities they committed in their savage mode of warfare, culminated in 1778 in the memorable massacre at Wyoming, and induced General Washington, in imitation of De Nonville, to send an

* N. Y. Historical Coll., 2d series, vol. 2, p. 180.
† The Genesee. In Seneca, Je-nis'-hi-yuh, or *beautiful, pleasant valley.*

army for their chastisement. The famous expedition under General Sullivan was organized for this purpose, which, penetrating the heart of the Seneca country, resulted, for the time being, in their overthrow and complete dispersion. The proud and formidable nation fled, panic-stricken, from their "pleasant valley," abandoned their villages, and sought British protection under the guns of Fort Niagara. They never, as a nation, resumed their ancient seats along the Genesee, but sought and found a new home on the secluded banks and among the basswood forests of the Buffalo Creek,* whence they had driven the Neutral Nation one hundred and thirty years before.

I have thus, with as much brevity as the nature of my subject would admit, noticed the aboriginal races that preceded us in the occupancy of this region. I consider this not an inappropriate introduction to a historical sketch of the most prominent localities on the Niagara frontier, and of the various names by which they have been known.

On the 6th day of December, 1678, La Salle, in his brigantine of ten tons, doubled the point where Fort Niagara now stands, and anchored in the sheltered waters of the river.† The prosecution of his bold enterprise at that inclement season, involving the exploration of a vast and unknown country, in vessels built on the way, indicates the indomitable energy and self-reliance of the intrepid discoverer. His crew consisted of sixteen persons, under the immediate command of the Sieur de la Motte. "*Te Deum laudamus!*" chanted the grateful Franciscans as they entered the noble river.

* Do'-syo-wä.
† Hennepin, p. 74.

The strains of that ancient hymn of the church, as they rose from the deck of the adventurous bark and echoed from shore and forest, must have startled the watchful Senecas with the unusual sound, as they gazed upon their strange visitors. Never before had white man, so far as history tells us, ascended the river. On its borders the roving Indian still contended for supremacy with the scarce wilder beasts of the forest. All was yet primitive and unexplored. Dense woods overhung the shore, except at the site of the present fort, or near the foot of the portage above, where a few temporary cabins sheltered some fishing-parties of the Senecas. The stream in which the French were now anchored, they called by its Indian name, NIAGARA. It is the oldest of all the local geographical terms which have come down to us from the aborigines. It was not at first thus written by the English, for with them it passed through almost every possible alphabetical variation before its present orthography was established.* We find its germ in the *On-gui-aah-ra* of the Neutral Nation as given by Father L' Allemant, in a letter dated in 1641, at the mission station of *Sainte Marie*.† In describing his visit to that people, he says: " From their first village, " which is about 40 leagues southerly from *Sainte Marie*, " it is four days' travel in a south-easterly direction, to " where the celebrated river of the Neutral Nation " empties into Lake Ontario. On the west and not on " the eastern side of said river, are the principal villages " of that nation. There are three or four on the eastern

---

* *Thirty-nine* different modes of spelling *Niagara* are enumerated by Dr. O. Callaghan. N. Y. Colonial Doc., Index volume. p. 465.

† *Sainte Marie* was located on the eastern shore of Lake Huron. Relation des Jesuits, 1639 40, p. 43.

"side, extending from east to west toward the Eries or
"Cat Nation. This river," he adds, "is that by which
"our great lake of the Hurons is discharged, after
"having emptied into Lake Erie, or lake of the Cat
"Nation, and it takes the name of *On-gui-aah-ra*, until
"it empties into the Ontario or St. Louis Lake."*

The name of the river next occurs on Sanson's map
of Canada, published in Paris in 1657, where it is spelled
"*Ongiara*." Its first appearance as *Niagara*, is on Coronelli's map, published in Paris in 1688. From that
time to the present, the French have been consistent in
their orthography, the numerous variations alluded to,
occurring only among the English writers. The word
was probably derived from the Mohawks, through whom
the French had their first intercourse with the Iroquois.†
Some controversy has existed concerning its signification. It is probably the same both in the Neutral and
Mohawk languages, as they were kindred dialects of one
generic tongue. The Mohawks affirm it to mean *neck*,
in allusion to its connecting the two lakes. The corres-
ponding Seneca name‡ was always confined by the
Iroquois to the section of the river below the Falls, and
to Lake Ontario. That portion of the river above the
Falls§ being sometimes called by one of their names for
Lake Erie.‖

The name was sometimes applied by the early his-
torians not only to the river, but to a defensive work

* Relation, 1641, p. 71.

† The Mohawks pronounce it Nyah'-ga-rah', with the primary accent on
the first syllable, and the second on the last.

‡ Nyah'-gaah. The signification of this Seneca word is lost. It is probably derived from the name conferred by the Neutral Nation.

§ N. Y. Colonial Documents, vol. V., p. 800, and IX, p. 999.

‖ Gai-gwääh-gëh.

and group of Indian cabins, which stood at or near the site of the present village of Lewiston. In the year 1678, La Salle constructed at this point a cabin of palisades to serve as a magazine or storehouse. In order to allay the jealousies which the work excited among the Senecas, he sent an embassy to *Tegarondies*, the principal village of the confederacy, then located on what is now known as Boughton Hill, near Victor, in Ontario county. They reached it in five days, after a march in mid-winter of thirty-two leagues, on snow-shoes, during which they subsisted only on parched corn. There they found the Jesuits, *Garnier* and *Raffeix*, who had been resident missionaries since 1669. A council was held with the Senecas and presents interchanged, but without favorable result. The French retraced their steps to their camp on the river, worn out with the hardships of the way, and glad to exchange their meagre diet for the delicious white fish just then in season.

No regular defensive work was constructed in the vicinity, until De Nonville, on his return from the expedition before alluded to, fortified the tongue of land or angle lying between the lake and the river embracing the site of the present fort. The French General describes it as "the most beautiful, pleasing and advantageous position on the whole lake." As early as 1686, he had proposed to his government to erect a stone fortress at this point, sufficient for a garrison of five hundred men, but received no favorable response. Many difficulties were now encountered in its construction. As the place was barren of suitable wood, palisades were cut at a distance, floated to the adjacent beach, and drawn up with great labor to the top of the bank. The work was finally completed, and called, after its founder, Fort De Nonville. It subsequently appears on some of the maps as *Fort Conty*, after a prince of that name, who was a patron of *Tonti*, one of La Salle's companions, but Niagara soon became its exclusive and more appropriate designation. De Nonville left in the fort a garrison of one hundred men, who were compelled by sickness to abandon it the following season, after having partially destroyed it. They left many of its buildings in an habitable condition, as may be learned from a curious inventory and statement drawn up at the time of the evacuation.* No measures appear to have been taken for its reconstruction until 1725, when, by consent of the Iroquois, it was commenced in stone, and finished the following year. The "old mess-house" is a relic of that era.

The French, having through the influence of *Joncaire* obtained the consent of the Senecas, rebuilt their storehouse at Lewiston in 1719–20. It formed a block-house forty feet long, by thirty wide, inclosed with palisades, musket proof, and pierced with port-holes. Around this nucleus gathered a cluster of ten Seneca cabins, and patches of corn, beans, squashes and melons were soon under cultivation. Father Charlevoix visited the spot in 1721, while on his extensive tour along the lakes, and has left quite an exaggerated description of the ridge at Lewiston, which he calls "a frightful mountain, that hides itself in the clouds, on which the Titans might attempt to scale the heavens!"†

The block-house must have soon fallen to decay, for

* N. Y. Colonial Docs., vol. 9, p. 386.

† Charlevoix's Journal, vol. 2., p. 345.

we find Louis XV. proposing to rebuild it in 1727,* but the project was abandoned the next year.

This locality was always considered an important point in the early history of the Niagara frontier. Here was the commencement of the *Portage* around the Falls, where all the goods in process of transportation between the lakes underwent transhipment. The traveled road pursued, as now, a zigzag course up the mountain ridge, but the heavy goods were raised or lowered in a sliding car or cradle, moved on an inclined plane by a windlass. The remains of the old tramway were visible at a late period, and possibly may still be seen. The ascent of the ledge at this point was so difficult, that long before the railway was constructed, the Senecas had given it a name which signifies, literally, "walking on all fours,"† in allusion to the postures assumed by the French and Indians while climbing the steep acclivity under their heavy burdens. Hennepin calls it "the three mountains," (*trois montagnes*),‡ in allusion to the high river-bank and the two terraces above it, which form the mountain ridge. When *Kalm* arrived there in 1750, he found one of the *Joncaires* still a resident. Over two hundred Senecas were then employed in carrying furs over the portage, at the rate of twenty pence a pack for the entire distance.§ There were three warehouses at the foot of the ridge in 1759, and one at its summit, all used for storing the goods *in transitu*.

Opposite Fort Niagara, on the Canada side of the river, is "MISSISSAUGA POINT," so called after one of the

* N. Y. Colonial Documents, vol. 9, p. 964.

† Duh'-jih-heh'-o'n.

‡ Hennepin, p. 113.

§ Kalm's letter in Annual Register, vol. 2, p. 389.

Algonkin tribes that formerly resided in the vicinity.*
The adjacent village of NIAGARA was known in 1780, by
the name of Butlersbury, after Colonel Butler of Wyoming notoriety.† It was afterward called Newark, after
the place of that name in New Jersey, and West Niagara
and British Niagara. In 1792 it became the residence
of the Lieutenant-Governor of Canada, and in the autumn of that year, the first session of the Parliament of
the Upper Province was held there. It is an older
settlement than any on the eastern side of the river, and
boasted a weekly newspaper as early as 1795. About
one mile above Newark, a defensive work was built by
the British, at the close of the last century, called FORT
GEORGE. Between this and the river was a storehouse,
bearing the high-sounding name of Navy Hall, and near
the latter the residence of Lieutenant-Governor Simcoe.

QUEENSTON, so called in honor of Queen Charlotte,
had no earlier name, though the locality was frequently
noticed by the first explorers. *Hennepin* speaks of it
as "the Great Rock,"‡ referring to an immense mass,
which, becoming detached from the brow of the mountain, had fallen into the river below. It is now plainly
visible under the western end of the lower Suspension
bridge.

The DEVIL'S HOLE and the WHIRLPOOL are not noticed by any of the early travelers. The former is more
particularly celebrated as the scene of a well known
bloody tragedy in 1763. Its Seneca name signifies,
" the cleft rocks."§ The BLOODY RUN, which falls over

* N. Y. Colonial Documents, vol. 5, p. 589.

† Gilbert's Narrative, p. 52. Col. Butler died in 1796. Merritt's MS.

‡ La grosse roche. Hennepin, p. 113.

§ Dyus-c̣ä̱'-nyah-gọh. The river-bank is *cleft* by the action of the Bloody
Run.

the precipice at this point, derives its present name from the same tragic occurrence, though the Indians have no term to distinguish it from the Devil's Hole. Their name for the Whirlpool means, literally, "the current goes round."*

It has already been stated, that the Indians, whom Cartier met in the Gulf of St. Lawrence in 1535, alluded, in their description of the interior, to a "CATARACT and portage," at the western extremity of Lake Ontario. This is the first historical notice of NIAGARA FALLS. Seventy-eight years afterward, Champlain published an account of his voyages in Canada, illustrated by a map of the country, on which the several lakes, as far west as Lake Huron, are laid down, though in very erroneous outline.† It distinctly shows the river Niagara, interrupted by a waterfall, and intersected by an elevation of land, answering to the mountain ridge at Lewiston. It contains no specific name for the cataract, but calls it "*Saut d' eau*," or waterfall. Champlain describes it as "so very high that many kinds of fish are stunned in "its descent."

The next notice of the cataract is by the Jesuit Father *Ragueneau*, who, in a letter to the Superior of the Missions at Paris, dated in 1648, says, "north of the Eries "is a great lake, about two hundred leagues in circum- "ference, called *Erié*, formed by the discharge of the "*mer-douce*, or Lake Huron, and which falls into a third "lake, called Ontario, over a *cataract* of frightful height."‡

Hennepin is the first who published a detailed description of this remarkable waterfall. He first saw it in the

---

* Dyu-no'-wa-da-se'.

† Edition of 1632.

‡ Jesuit Relation, 1648, p. 46.

winter of 1678-9, and accompanies his description by an
engraved sketch,* evidently drawn from memory, as it
embraces a bird's eye view of the whole river, as far as
Lake Erie, with the *Griffin* in the distance. The two
falls, with Goat Island between, and Table Rock, are
very well delineated, though the height is very much
exaggerated. A group of Frenchmen, viewing the cataract from the American side, are represented as stop-
ping their ears to shut out the deafening sound.

No doubt the Falls were visited at an earlier date by
numerous traders and voyageurs, but no record of the
fact exists. The Niagara was not a favorite route to the
far west, the Ottawa being shorter and safer for a canoe
voyage, an easy portage connecting its head-waters with
Lake Huron. The fatiguing transit around the Falls,
and the hostility of the warlike Iroquois, were formidable obstacles to the more southern course.

The Seneca name of the Cataract† signifies "the
place of the high fall." They never call it Niagara, nor
by any similar term, neither does that word signify in
their language "thunder of waters," as affirmed by School-
craft.‡ Such a meaning would be eminently poetic, but
truth is of higher importance.

The picturesque ISLANDS which add so much to the
beauty and unrivaled scenery of the Falls, must have
challenged the admiration and stimulated the curiosity
of the early visitor. Equally attractive at all seasons,
whether arrayed in summer verdure, colored with the
tints of autumn, or clothed in the crystal robes of win-

* Hennepin, p. 116.

† Det-gah'-skoh-ses. See appendix.

‡ Tour to the Lakes. p. 32.

ter,* they reposed like fairy creations, amid the turmoil of the impetuous rapids, isolated and apparently secure from human intrusion or profanation. Traditions exist of early Indian visits to the larger one, which are confirmed by a deposit of human bones discovered near its head. The access was from the river above, through the still water between the divided currents. Judge Porter first landed there in 1806, and found several dates carved on a beech, the earliest of which was 1769. He purchased the entire group from the State in 1816, and during the following year built the first bridge which connected them with the main land. Stedman had cleared a small field near the upper end of the largest, and colonized it with a few animals, including a venerable goat. The latter was the only survivor of the severe winter of 1779–80, in commemoration of which the island received its present name. The Boundary Commissioners under the Treaty of Ghent, gave to it the more poetic title, Iris Island, but the earlier one was destined to prevail.

JUDGE PORTER was one of the earliest settlers at the Falls, having erected his first dwelling there in 1809–10. He foresaw the unrivaled advantages of the position, and secured, at an early day, the fee of a large tract of land in the vicinity. In addition to his dwelling, he erected mills, probably on the site where Lieutenant DePeyster built a saw-mill in 1767, and which Stedman subsequently occupied for the same purpose. He also constructed a rope-walk for the manufacture of rigging

---

* Those who visit Niagara in summer only, see but half its beauties. In winter, the spray, congealed by frost on every tree, bush and rock, glitters with diamond lustre in the sunlight, while, in the gulf below, cones, pyramids and towers, immense stalactites and frost work in every variety of form, are produced by the falling waters.

for Porter, Barton & Co.,* who were then the principal carriers on the portage, and owned or controlled nearly all the trading vessels on the two lakes and river. All kinds of rigging, including cables of the largest size required, were here manufactured. Much of the hemp they used, was raised by the Wadsworths on the Genesee flats. Such was the scarcity of men in the then new country, that the Judge was indebted to Capt. Armisted of Fort Niagara, for a company of 100 men, to assist him in raising the heavy frame of his mill. It proved to be expensive aid, for the soldiers stripped his garden of all its fruit, then very fine and abundant. All his buildings, embracing dwellings, mills and rope-walks, shared in the general conflagration on the frontier in 1813.

The village on the American side of the Falls, has been known as Grand Niagara and Manchester, and is now incorporated under the name of Niagara Falls.

FORT SCHLOSSER, was named after Captain Joseph Schlosser, a native of Germany, who served in the British army in the campaign against Fort Niagara in 1759.† Sir William Johnson found him at Schlosser in 1761. He must have remained until the autumn of 1763, for it is stated by *Loskiel* and *Heckewelder*,‡ that he arrived at Philadelphia in January, 1764, having just returned from Niagara with a detachment from General Gage's army. Heckewelder pays a high tribute to his humanity and manly qualities. §

The earlier names of the Post were, *Fort du Portage, Little Fort* and *Little Niagara.*|| It was not built until

* This well known firm was composed of Augustus Porter, Peter B. Porter, Benjamin Barton, and Joseph Annin.

† N. Y. Colonial Documents, vol. x, p. 731, n. 5.

‡ Loskiel's Missions, p. 222.

§ Heckewelder's Narrative, p. 83.

|| N. Y. Colonial Docs. vol. vii, p. 621.

1750. In the summer of that year, the younger *Chabert Joncaire*, informed the Senecas that the French Government intended to build a Fort at the south end of the Portage, above Niagara Falls. The project was carried into effect the same season, and we find that *Joncaire Clauzonne*, brother of *Chabert*, was appointed its commandant.* In 1755, it was called Fisher's Battery.† When Sir William Johnson invested Fort Niagara in 1759, *Chabert Joncaire* seems to have been in command at Fort Schlosser, his brother *Clauzonne* being then with him. On the fall of the former fortress, Fort Schlosser was burnt, and its garrison withdrawn to the Chippewa river, on the opposite side. It must have been speedily rebuilt by the British, for we find Captain Schlosser stationed there soon after in command of a garrison. The fort then consisted of an enclosure of upright palisades, protecting a few store-houses and barracks. Alexander Henry, who visited it in 1764, calls it a "stockaded post."‡ The plough has obliterated all traces of its existence, save some inequalities in the surface where it stood, plainly visible from the neighboring railroad. The tall, antique chimney which rises from the adjacent buildings, is not, as generally supposed, a relic of the fort, but of barracks, constructed by the French, and destroyed by *Joncaire*, on his retreat in 1759. The same chimney was subsequently used by the English when they re-established the post. The dwelling they erected was afterward occupied by Stedman, who was a contractor at the portage from 1760 until after the peace of 1783. He probably remained until after Fort Niagara was

* Lewis Evans' map.
† N. Y. Colonial Docs. vol. vi. p. 608, 706.
‡ Travels. p. 183.

delivered to the United States by the British authorities in 1796, when he removed to the Canadian side. He left his "improvements" in charge of a man known as Jesse Ware. They are described by a visitor at that early day, as consisting of seventeen hundred acres, about one-tenth partially cleared, an indifferent dwelling, a fine barn, saw-mill, and a well fenced apple orchard containing twelve hundred trees.*

There appear to have been three brothers by the name of Stedman, John, Philip and William. The traveler Maude, found John at Schlosser in 1800. While master of the portage, he had command of the wagons and their escort, at the time of the massacre at the Devil's Hole in September, 1763, before alluded to. It was a return train which had been transporting supplies from Fort Niagara for the use of the garrison at Detroit. Only three persons escaped; a drummer-boy who lodged in a tree as he fell over the precipice, a wounded driver, who lay concealed in some evergreens near by, and Stedman himself, who, being well mounted, forced his way through the Indians and escaped amid a shower of bullets, to Fort Schlosser. Two companies of troops that were stationed at Lewiston, hearing the firing, hastened to their relief. The wily Senecas, anticipating the re-inforcement, lay in ambush, and all but eight fell by the rifle or the tomahawk. The entire garrison of Fort Niagara was then despatched to the scene, but arrived only to find the ghastly and mangled remained of their slaughtered comrades.

The Seneca Sachem, *John Blacksmith*, informed the writer that the party which made the attack, were young warriors from the Genesee, who, instigated by the French

* Voyage par Hector St. John, vol. ii, p. 153.

traders, secretly organized the expedition under the leadership of Farmer's Brother, without the knowledge of their chiefs. Eighty scalps, including those of six officers, were their bloody trophies.

The Senecas, attributing the preservation of Stedman to some miraculous interposition, and believing he wore a charmed life, conferred upon him the name of "Stone Giant."* The story that they gave him all the land lying between the river and the line of his flight, embracing about five thousand acres, is undoubtedly a fiction. The pretended grant was the foundation of the "Stedman claim," which was subsequently urged upon the State authorities with much pertinacity. If really made, it seems never to have been ratified by the Senecas, for at a formal treaty held with them by Sir William Johnson at Johnson Hall, in April of the following year, signed by *Farmer's Brother* and *Old Smoke*, it was not only not alluded to, but on the contrary, a strip of land four miles wide on the east side of the river, commencing at Lake Ontario and extending southerly to Gill creek, embracing the entire Stedman claim, was ceded in perpetuity to his Brittanic Majesty.† Stedman petitioned the Legislature in 1800, to confirm the pretended grant, but without success. He recites in his memorial, that he took the possession of the premises in 1760, and soon after met with a great loss from the Indians; that as a compensation therefor, the chiefs gave him a deed of the tract containing 4,983 acres, and which he had continued to improve for forty years; that the deed had perished with the papers of Sir William Johnson, which had been buried in an iron chest at Johnson Hall. A

* Gä-nas-squah.

† N. Y. Colonial Docs. vol. vii. p. 621.

bill passed the Assembly, giving him the land he had actually improved, but it failed in the Senate. The buildings on the premises had suffered much from decay as early as 1800, and the adjacent fort was in ruins. The old orchard was still productive, the overplus yield bringing $500 in a single season, but the boys, crossing from the Canada side, plundered most of the fruit.*

The PORTAGE ROAD commenced at the Lewiston landing, and followed the river until it reached the small depression just north of the present Suspension Bridge. Diverging from this, it intersected the river a short distance above the Stedman house, and followed its bank for about forty rods to the fort above. Midway between the house and fort, were a dock, a ware-house, and a group of square-timbered, whitewashed log-cabins, used by the teamsters, boatmen and engagees connected with the portage.†

About half a mile below the Stedman house, near the head of the present hydraulic canal, was the OLD FRENCH LANDING, where goods were transhipped when only canoes were used, and where the portage road terminated before Fort Schlosser was built. All along the road between the fort and Lewiston, block-houses were erected about a mile apart, to protect the teams from disasters such as had occurred at the Devil's Hole. The remains of some of these were quite recently in existence.

Judge Porter leased the Stedman farm from the State in 1805, the agent, Ware, being still in possession. He was ejected with some difficulty. Legal steps were taken, but owing to the unsettled state of the country, and the difficulty of executing process in a region so

* Maude's Niagara, p. 146.
† Manuscript letter of Hon. A. S. Porter.

remote from civilization, recourse was had to *Judge Lynch*, before possession was finally obtained.* Judge Porter occupied the dwelling during the years 1806–7 and 8, when he removed to the Falls. He was succeeded by Enos Boughton, one of the first pioneers on the Holland Purchase, who opened a tavern for the accommodation of early visitors to the Falls, and travelers en route for the great West. It became the Head Quarters in all that region, for military musters, general trainings and fourth of July celebrations. The buildings were destroyed by the British in December, 1813, but the old chimney was suffered to remain, conspicuous among the surrounding ruins, a weather beaten memorial of the ruthless desolation of war.

GILL CREEK, so named from its diminutive size, and called also *Cayuga Creek*,† and *Stedman's Creek*, derives its only importance from being named as a boundary in some of the early Indian treaties.‡

CHIPPEWA CREEK, nearly opposite Fort Schlosser, is called by the Senecas *Jo-no-dak*, signifying "shallow water," probably referring to an old fording place at the mouth of the creek. *Pouchot*, in his narrative of the siege of Fort Niagara, calls it *Chenondac*, evidently the same name, and describes its banks as abounding in fine timber, suitable for ship building.§ It was named *Chippewa*, after the *Ojibway*—otherwise called *Mississauga* Indians, who formerly lived on its banks. The Canadian Government by proclamation in 1792, gave it the name of *Welland* river, but it did not pass into general use.

---

* Manuscript letter of Hon. A. S. Porter.

† Savary's Journal, p. 360.

‡ Treaty at Canandaigua in 1794.

§ Pouchot, vol. iii, p. 174.

The earliest notice of the stream is found in the narrative of Father *Hennepin*, who, while seeking a site suitable for building the *Griffin*, encamped on its banks in the winter of 1678–9. He says, "it runs from the west, and empties into the Niagara within a league above the great fall." He found the snow a foot deep, and was obliged to remove it before building his camp-fire. The narrative incidentally mentions the abundance of deer and wild turkeys that were found in the vicinity.*

The Seneca name for NAVY ISLAND, signifies: "The big canoe island."† This is in allusion to the vessels built there by the French at an early day, for use on the lakes. Hence the French name, *Isle-la-Marine*, and the English name, *Navy Island*. It contains about 300 acres. A tradition still exists among the Senecas that a brass cannon was mounted on one of the vessels.‡ It was there the French reinforcements arrived from Venango for the garrison at Fort Niagara, during its siege by Sir William Johnson. The English built two vessels on the island in 1764, one of which was accidentally burned there in 1767. The island has become more celebrated in modern times as the rendezvous of the Patriot forces during the Canadian rebellion of 1838.

GRAND ISLAND is called by the Senecas, "The Great Island."‡ It is mentioned by *Hennepin* under its present name.§ At its northern extremity, in a sheltered bay, the remains of two vessels may now be seen at low water, which, tradition says, belonged to the French, and

---

* Hennepin, p. 75.

† Ga-o'-wah-go-waah.

‡ A brass six-pounder was placed on one of the British vessels in 1764. Governor Simcoe's manuscript letter to Col. England.

‡ Ga-we'-not.

§ Hennepin, p. 49.

were burnt at the time Fort Niagara capitulated, to prevent their falling into the hands of the English. This has given origin to the name, *Burnt Ship Bay.* I have been unable, however, to find any historical verification of this tradition. Sir William Johnson, while on his way West in August, 1761, encamped for the night on the west side of this island, at the mouth of a creek now called Six Mile Creek, which he describes as a fine position, affording an eligible situation for a house, and a good harbor for boats. He called it *Point Pleasant,* a name, the origin of which certainly entitles it to perpetuation. The Baronet makes special mention of the fine oaks with which the island abounded.*

CAYUGA CREEK was so named by the Senecas. On the 22d day of January, 1679, La Salle and his companions constructed a dock at its mouth, and laid the keel of the first vessel built on our western waters. The site chosen was just south of the stream, close to the river bank. The first bolt was driven on the 26th, and notwithstanding the attempts of the jealous Iroquois to burn the vessel, and to kill and entice away the workmen, its hull was completed the following spring. Blessed by the church, amid the strains of the *Te-deum,* the salvos of artillery, the shouts of the Frenchmen and the astonishment of the savages, it was launched and christened the *Griffin.* Casting anchor in the stream, the crew swung their hammocks on board, and awaited their supplies from Fort Frontenac, for the first time secure from the treacherous natives since their sojourn in the wilderness. With great difficulty they carried their provisions, munitions of war, and other necessaries, up the Mountain ridge and over the portage. Father

* Stone's Johnson, vol. ii, p. 45.

*Gabriel,** then 64 years old, went back and forth, engaged like the rest in the laborious task. Four men carried their largest anchor, and when overcome by the toil, were plied and refreshed with brandy.

The vessel was ready for the voyage the following August, when, fully equipped and armed, it ascended the river as far as the rapids near Lake Erie, and anchored above the head of Grand Island. While waiting for a favorable wind to aid in overcoming the powerful current, La Salle landed a party of his men on the Canadian shore, and planted some garden seeds for the benefit of those who should come after him. Thus our voyagers became the pioneer horticulturists of all this region.†

The rapids having been sounded by Father Hennepin, and reported navigable, the *Griffin* set sail on the 7th, the wind being fresh from the north-east, and aided by twelve of the crew at the tow-lines on shore, surmounted the current and entered the lake.

Again the *Te Deum* was chanted, their guns all discharged, and the vessel pursued its adventurous way westward, over waters as yet unvexed by the keel of commerce, pioneer of a fleet, whose present tonnage would compare favorably with what the whole world could then boast of. She arrived safely at Green Bay, but was lost on her return voyage with all on board.

In commemoration of this enterprise, the name of La Salle has been conferred upon the small village and post-office at the locality where the *Griffin* was built.

---

* Father Gabriel was the last scion of a noble Burgundian house. He had renounced the world and all its honors for the order of St. Francis. He perished the next year by the hand of the Kickapoos, on his way from Ft. Crevecœur to Green Bay.

† Hennepin, p. 118.

The same site was selected by the United States Government about the year 1804, for the construction of a small sloop of 50 tons burden, called the "Niagara," and used for conveying supplies to the western posts. It was subsequently purchased by Porter, Barton & Co., re-built at Black Rock, and named the "Nancy," after the wife of the late Benjamin Barton, one of the partners.* While bearing the latter name she was commanded by Captain Richard O'Neil, and went out of commission just before the war of 1812.

TONAWANDA CREEK was so called by the Senecas, after the rapids at their village a few miles above its mouth, it signifying literally, "a rough stream or current."† The French called it, *La riviere aux bois blancs*, or "white wood river." On the early maps it is called *Maskinongez*, that being the Chippewa name for the muskelunge, a fish once abundant in the stream.

The Senecas have a different name for TONAWANDA ISLAND. They call it, "The Small Island."‡ It contains less than 100 acres. Its upper end having a fine elevation above the surface of the river, was an occasional camping ground of the Senecas, before their final settlement in this region. *Philip Kenjockety* (hereafter more particularly noticed,) claims to have been born there, while his father's family, then residing on the Genesee, were on one of their annual hunting expeditions.

Two negro‧ brothers lived at an early day, at the mouth of CORNELIUS CREEK, just below Lower Black Rock. They were supposed to be runaway slaves. The

---

* Mrs. Barton was usually called Nancy, but her baptismal name was Agnes.

† Ta-no′-wan-deh.

‡ Ni-ga′-we-nąh′-ą-ąh.

elder was called by the Senecas "Rock Bass,"* on account of a red spot in one of his eyes, resembling that in the eye of the fish. Hence they called the creek, "the residence of Rock Bass."† He was shrewd and intelligent; became a trader in cattle with parties in Canada and at Fort Niagara; chose a wife among the Seneca maidens, and acquired considerable property. The notorious Ebenezer Allen married one of his daughters, and added her to his extensive harem on the Genesee. The younger negro was called *So-wak*, or "Duck." Both died more than half a century ago, leaving numerous descendants, some now living on the Tonawanda Reservation.

KENJOCKETY CREEK was not so named by the Senecas. They called it after a peculiar kind of wild grass, that grew near its borders.‡ The name "Kenjockety"§ was given by the whites, after an Indian family they found living on its banks. Its literal signification is "Beyond the Multitude." JOHN KONJOCKETY, the head of the family, was the son of a *Kah-kwa*, or Neutral Indian, whose father had been taken prisoner by the Senecas in the war which resulted in the extermination of his people. This occurred at the capture of one of the *Kah-kwa* villages, located on a branch of the Eighteen Mile Creek, near White's Corners in this county. His family wigwams were on the north bank of *Kenjockety Creek*, a little east of the present Niagara street. They obtained their water for domestic use from the river, then fordable at low water to Squaw Island. The creek still retains among the whites the name they first gave

† O-gah'-gwääh'-gëh.
* O-gah'-gwääh.
‡ Ga-noh'-gwaht-gëh.
§ Sgä-dyuh'-gwa-dih.

it—the Senecas adhering to the more ancient designation. The old chief must have been a man of more than ordinary consideration among his people. The Rev. Mr. Kirkland mentions him in the journal of his tour to Buffalo creek in 1788. He writes his name "*Skendyoughgwatti*," and styles him "the second man of influence and character among the Senecas at the Buffaloe."* His name is appended to a letter addressed to Governor George Clinton in 1789, remonstrating against some unauthorized sales of Indian lands.† The Hon. Augustus Porter, who surveyed the boundary line of the " Gore," between the Seneca Reservation and Lake Erie, stated to the writer that he was accompanied during the survey "by an old Indian named *Scaugh-juh-quatty*," who had been appointed by the Senecas to act with Red Jacket for that purpose. They indicated the edge of the swamp as the line for Judge Porter to follow, by preceding him from tree to tree, thereby carefully excluding what is now called "the Tifft farm," and the remainder of the *Flats*, as comparatively of no value. This will account for the zigzag course of the line in question.

Kenjockety continued to reside on the creek, until about the commencement of the present century, cultivating his corn-field on Squaw Island, and drawing abundant subsistence for himself and family from the river and the forest. The survey of the " Mile-strip" by the State authorities, and the arrival of the pioneers of Buffalo, disturbed his tranquil home, and compelled him to remove to the Reservation, where he finally settled on the bank of Buffalo creek, near the present iron bridge. Becoming dissipated in his old age, he perished

---

* Kirkland's Ms. Journal in N. Y. State Library.
† Indian Treaties, vol. ii, p. 331.

miserably by the roadside, from the effects of intoxication, while on his way home from Buffalo in October, 1808.

SQUAW ISLAND was called by the Senecas "a divided island,"* referring to its division by the marshy creek known as "Smugger's Run."† It was presented by the Nation to Captain Parish, their favorite agent and interpreter, as an acknowledgment, says the record, of his many services in their behalf. The gift was ratified by the Legislature in 1816, though the Captain was required to pay the State at the rate of two dollars per acre before he obtained his patent. He sold the island to Henry F. Penfield, Esq., in 1823. Captain Parish and his colleague, Captain Jones, had each previously obtained a donation of a mile square on the river, now known as the Jones and Parish Tracts, and lying within the present bounds of our city. The Legislature was induced to make this grant, by that touching and effective petition dictated by Farmer's Brother, which has been so often cited as a specimen of Indian eloquence.‡

BIRD ISLAND was originally several feet above the river level, rocky at its lower end, and partially covered with tall trees. It has entirely disappeared, the rock which composed it having been used in the construction of the Black Rock pier. Its Seneca name,§ signifies "Rocky Island." It was called "Bird Island" by the whites, because of the multitude of gulls and other aquatic birds that frequented it at certain seasons.‖

* De-dyo′-we-nǫ′-guh-dǫh.

† Philip Kenjockety stated to the writer that he has often passed through this creek in his canoe, on his way to Canada.

‡ Copied in Turner's Holland Land Company purchase, p. 291.

§ Dyos-dä-o-ċǫħ.

‖ Campbell's Life of Clinton, p. 128.

BLACK ROCK, being a convenient crossing place on the Niagara, became an important locality at an early day. Its history has been fully illustrated in an able and interesting paper entitled "The Old Ferry," read before this Society.* Its Seneca name, signifying "rocky bank,"† is a compound word, embracing also the idea of a place where the lake rests upon or against a rocky bank. Its English name comes from the dark corniferous limestone which outcrops at this locality, and underlying the bed of the outlet, composes the dangerous reef at the head of the rapids.

Prior to the commencement of the present century, the usual route between Buffalo Creek and the Falls, was on the Canada side, crossing at Black Rock. The Rev. Samuel Kirkland traveled it in 1788, and the Duke of Liancourt in 1795.

FORT ERIE was originally built by Col. Bradstreet, some distance below the present structure, while on his expedition against the Western Indians in the summer of 1764. He states in a letter to General Amhert, still unpublished,‡ that "when he arrived at the locality he "found no harbor. That vessels were compelled to lie "at anchor in the open lake, exposed to every storm, "and liable to be lost. In addition to this, they were "obliged to send more than twenty miles for their load-"ing; that on examining the north shore, he found a "suitable place to secure the vessels by the help of a "wharf just above the rapids. A Post," he adds, "is "now building there, and all that can, will be done "toward finishing it this season." He further says, that "to avoid giving offense to the Seneca savages, to

* By C. Norton, Esq.   † Dyos-dääh´-ga-eh.
‡ Bradstreet's manuscripts. N. Y. S. Library.

"whom the land belongs, I have desired Sir William
" Johnson to ask it of them, and they have granted it."
This letter is dated August 4th, 1764. The treaty between Sir William and the Senecas bears date two days
after, at Fort Niagara, and cedes to His Majesty all the
land, four miles wide, on each side of the river, between
Fort Schlosser and the rapids of Lake Erie. The
islands in the river were excepted by the Indians, and
bestowed upon Sir William "as a proof," says the record, " of their regard, and of their knowledge of the
" trouble he has had with them from time to time." Sir
William accepted the gift, but, like a good subject, hum-
bly laid it as an offering at the feet of his sovereign.*

. The foundations of the present fort were laid in
1791.† It must have been a rude fortification as originally constructed, for the Duke of Liancourt describes
it in 1795, as a cluster of buildings surrounded with
rough, crazy palisades, destitute of ramparts, covered
ways, or earthworks. Outside of the fort were a few log
houses for the shelter of the officers, soldiers and workmen. There was also a large government warehouse,
with an overhanging story pierced with loop-holes for
the use of musketry.‡ The stone fort, a portion of
which still remains, was built in 1806, in the form of a
quadrangle, and subsequently enlarged to more formidable dimensions. Its Indian name signifies " The place
of hats."§ Seneca tradition relates, as the origin of the
name, that in olden time, soon after the first visit of the
white man, a battle occurred on the lake between a
party of French in batteaux and Indians in canoes.

* N. Y. Colonial Documents, vol. vii, p. 647.

† Indian State Papers, vol. i, p. 160.

‡ Voyage par Liancourt, vol. ii, p. 4.

§ Gai-gwăăh-gĕh.

The latter were victorious, and the French boats were sunk and their occupants drowned. Their hats floated ashore where the fort was subsequently built, and attracting the attention of the Indians from their novelty, they called the locality " The place of hats."

In the summer of 1687, the Baron *La Hontan* ascended in his birchen canoe, the rapids of the Niagara into Lake Erie, on his way to the far West.* Appreciating with military eye this commanding locality, he recommended it to the French Government as suitable for a fort, and marked it "*Fort Supposé*" on the map which illustrates his journal. This is the earliest historical notice of the site of Buffalo. No attention appears to have been paid to the recommendation, and for more than a century it remained in undisturbed repose, its solitudes unbroken by the axe of the woodman, or the tread of advancing civilization. Voyageurs, traders and missionaries passed and re-passed on the river, but make no mention of even an Indian encampment. Nor does Sir William Johnson, who ascended the outlet into the lake on his way west in August, and returned in October, 1761.†

It has already been mentioned that the Senecas fled to Fort Niagara in 1779 before the invading forces of General Sullivan, and settled the following year on the banks of the Buffalo Creek. A single survivor of that fugitive band is now living on the Cattaraugus Reservation, in the person of the venerable *Philip Kenjockety*, a son of the *John Kenjockety* previously mentioned. When the writer saw him in June last, he appeared strong and vigorous, being employed at the time in piling hemlock

* La Hontan, English ed., vol. i, p. 82.

† Journal in Stone's Johnson, vol. ii, pp. 451 and 470.

bark. His entire dress was a loose cotton shirt, and the customary Indian leggings. He presented a fine specimen of the native Indian of the old school, a class now almost extinct. He claimed to be 100 years old, and a little examination into his personal history furnished proof of his correctness. It appeared that he was about fifteen at the time of Sullivan's expedition, and resided at Nunda. He well remembered the flight of the Senecas on that occasion, when he drove a horse to Fort Niagara. The fugitives arrived there in the month of September, and remained in its neighborhood and under its protection during the following winter. The season was the most inclement known for many years, so much so that the river opposite the fort was frozen from the 7th of January until the following March, and many of the Senecas perished from exposure and starvation before the ensuing spring. Brant made strenuous efforts during the winter to induce the Senecas to locate in Canada under the protection of the British Government. The Mohawks and a few from the other tribes yielded to his solicitations, but *Kenjockety's* father, who was intimately acquainted with the superior advantages of Western New York, successfully opposed the Mohawk chieftain, and prevailed upon the remainder to settle in the region watered by the Buffalo, Cattaraugus and Tonawanda creeks.

While listening to the eventful narrative of the aged Seneca, the writer could scarcely realize that the man was still living, who not only resided in this locality at the first advent of the white man, but who came here, with the Senecas themselves, to reap, by a permanent occupancy, the substantial fruits of their ancient conquests.

At the time of the arrival of the Senecas, the striking feature of this locality was the predominance of the linden or basswood over all the other trees of the forest. They fringed both borders of the creek, and spread their ample foliage over its fertile bottoms. Seneca tradition tells us, that in the season when the tree was in flower, the hunting-parties from the Genesee could hear, ere they reached the creek, the hum of the bee as it gathered, in countless swarms, its winter stores from the abundant blossoms. Michaux, the French naturalist who traveled through this region in 1807, states as a peculiarity of this locality, in his great work on the forest trees of America, that the basswood constituted two-thirds, and, in some localities, the whole of the forest between Batavia and New Amsterdam.* Early settlers say, that the peninsula, bounded by Main street, Buffalo Creek and the canal, embracing what is now intersected by Prime, Lloyd and Hanover streets, was almost exclusively covered with this tree. It was occasionally found more than eighty feet high and four feet in diameter. Its giant trunks furnished, at that convenient locality, a light and soft wood from which to fashion the Indian canoe, and a bark easily converted into various utensils useful in savage life. This bark formed the exclusive covering of the temporary huts, erected for the shelter of the hunting and fishing-parties that frequented this region. The Senecas, in conformity with their well-known custom, seized upon this marked peculiarity of the place, and conferred upon it a name, strikingly euphonious in their tongue, and meaning " The place of basswoods."†

* North American Sylva, vol. iii, p. 131.

† Do'-syo-w꞉. Also called Te-hos-e-ro-ron, in the treaty at Fort Stanwix, it being a variation, in Mohawk, of the Seneca name.

The origin of the name, BUFFALO, has already been so thoroughly discussed in and out of this Society, that no additional light can be thrown upon the subject. Its first occurrence is conceded to be in the narrative of the captivity and residence of the Gilbert family among the Senecas during the years 1780–81, which was published in 1784. It next occurs in the treaty at Fort Stanwix before alluded to. The Rev. Mr. Kirkland, in his journal of a visit to the Senecas in 1788,* speaks of their "village on the Buffaloe," and from that time the name appears to have passed into general use. The Holland Company endeavored to supplant it with the term "New Amsterdam," but our village fathers, with great good sense, rejected the substitute, together with the foreign names which the same company had imposed upon our streets.

The Senecas, with a few kindred Onondagas and Cayugas, on their arrival here, selected eligible locations along the borders of Buffalo Creek. The former chose the southern bank, and the level bottoms beyond the present iron bridge, east of what is now known as "Martin's Corners." The Onondagas went higher up, and established their wigwams on the elevated table land near where the southern Ebenezer village was subsequently located. The Cayugas settled north of the Onondagas, along that branch of the creek to which they gave their name.

In these localities the tribes were found, when the vanguard of emigration reached them, and here they remained, dividing their time between hunting, fishing, and the cultivation of the soil, until the encroachments of the white man diminished their game, and created a

* MS. journal in N. Y. State Library.

demand for their lands too eager and powerful to be resisted. We have seen, within a few years, the last of the Senecas abandon these ancient seats, some to locate on the adjacent Reservations, and others to seek "a wider hunting-ground" beyond the Mississippi.

They left the graves of their fathers in the possession of the white man, and how has he fulfilled the trust? A visit to yonder rude and neglected cemetery will furnish the answer. The violated grave of Red Jacket bears witness against us.* The remains of the chief, though rescued from the spoiler, are still, through fear of further profanation, denied the common rite of sepulture. The headstone of the " White Woman," carried away by piecemeal for relics by the curious, no longer tells the simple, touching story of her remarkable life. *Pollard* and *Young King* and *White Seneca*, and many others, whose names were once as household words among us, all rest in unmarked graves. They were the friends of the founders of our city, when the Indians were strong and the white man weak. Our conditions are now reversed. Having crowded the living from their ancient seats and pleasant hunting-grounds, shall we rob their graves and desecrate their ashes? One of their eloquent chiefs† has touchingly and reproachfully told us, " the bones of his people lie in exile in their own country." Would it not be an appropriate work for this Society to initiate measures for the permanent protection and preservation of their dead? The remains of such of their distin-

* Red Jacket's grave was robbed of its remains in 1852. His family recovered and still retain them. They are preserved in a chest on the Cattaraugus Reservation.

† De jih´-non-da-weh-hoh. *The Pacificator.* (Dr. Wilson.)

guished chiefs as can now be identified, should be removed to some consecrated spot in our new cemetery. There, on the quiet banks of the Ga-noh'-gwaht-geh, in the shadow of the native forest, they could repose in security. There the dust of our antagonistic races might commingle undisturbed, until the final summons shall call alike, from the ostentatious mausoleum of the white man and the humble grave of the Indian, the innumerable dead to one common Judgment.

APPENDIX.

The following list embraces many of the early names that have been applied to some of our great lakes and rivers, and to a few prominent localities along their borders. Several of inferior note, though of more local interest, are also given. The great diversity that has existed in the mode of spelling the geographical terms of the Iroquois, has given rise to much confusion and uncertainty. This has induced the writer to adopt, in reducing the Seneca names to English orthography, the admirable system invented by the Rev. Asher Wright, of the Cattaraugus Mission. That able missionary has published in the Seneca language, which he speaks and writes fluently, several works of much interest to the philologist, the fruit of his many years of successful labor among that people. The acknowledgments of the writer are justly due to him for his assistance in determining the orthography and signification of many of the names that occur in these pages ; also to Dr. Peter Wilson, Nathaniel T. Strong and Nicholson H. Parker, all highly intelligent and cultivated members of the Iroquois family.

The following is the key to Mr. Wright's system. If the sounds of the letters and accents are strictly observed, a close approximation to the correct pronunciation will be reached.

a sounded like a in fall.

ä sounded like a in hat.

e sounded like e in they.

ĕ sounded like e in bet.

i sounded like i in machine.

ï sounded like i in fit.

o sounded like o in note.

ò intermediate between o in note and o in move.

u sounded like u in push.

ai sounded like i in pine.

iu sounded like u in pure.

ch always soft, as in chin.

ħ sounded like the h in the interjection oh ! when impatiently uttered ; approaching the sound of k, though not quite reaching it.

When h comes after t or s it is separately sounded.

A mark underneath a vowel, thus ɋ, represents a nasal sound.

There are no silent letters.

A repeated vowel only lengthens the sound.

LAKE ONTARIO.

Lac des Entouhonorons. I Champlain, 1632, p. 336. So called after a
nation living south of the lake.
St. Louis. Champlain ed., 1632. Rel., 1640-41, p. 49.
Des Iroquois. Relation des Jesuits, 1635, p. 121.
Lo Mer Douce. "*The Fresh Sea.*" Relation, 1639-40, p. 130.
Ontario. "*Beautiful Lake.*" Hennepin, p. 31. Relation, 1640-41, p. 49.
Skanadario. "*Beautiful Lake.*" Hennepin, p. 42.
Cadarackui. Colden, xvi.
Frontenac. Hennepin, p. 40.

LAKE ERIE.

Erié. Relation, 1641, p. 71.
Du Chat. "*Cat Lake.*" Sanson's Map of 1651.
De Conty. Coronelli's Map of 1688.
Oswego. N. Y. Colonial Documents v, p. 694.

LAKE HURON.

La Mer Douce. "*The Fresh Sea.*" Champlain, appendix, p. 8.
Attigouantan. Champlain i, p. 324.
Karegnondi. Sanson's Map of 1657.
Des Hurons. Relation, 1670-71, map.
D' Orleans. Coronelli's Map of 1688.
Quatoghe. Colden, xvi.
Caniatare. Colden, xvi.

LAKE MICHIGAN.

Des Puants. Champlain, 1632.
Des Illinois. Relation, 1669-70. Marquette's Map, 1674.
St. Joseph. Father Allouez in 1675.
Dauphin. Coronelli's Map of 1688.
Michigonong. Hennepin, p. 53.

LAKE SUPERIOR.

Le Grand Lac. "*The great Lake.*" Champlain, 1632.
Superieur. "*Upper Lake.*" Relation, 1660, p. 9.
De Tracy. Relation, 1667, p. 4.
De Condé. Le Clercq, p. 137.

NIAGARA FALLS.

Saut d'eau. "*Waterfall.*" Champlain's Map, 1613.

Onguiaahra. Relation, 1640–41, p. 65. Applied to river only.

Ongiara. Sanson's Map of 1651. Ducreux, 1660.

Unghiara. Bancroft's U. S., vol. iii, p. 128.

Och-ni-a-gara. Evans's Map, 1755.

Iagara. Colden's Five Nations, appendix, p. 15.

O-ni-a-ga-rah. Colden's Five Nations, p. 79.

O-ny-a-kar-rah. Macauley's N. Y., vol. ii, p. 177.

Tgah-sgoh'-so-wa-nǎh. "*The Great Fall.*" Common Seneca name. Sometimes also called—

Det-gah'-sgoh-ses. "*The High Fall.*"

MISCELLANEOUS SENECA NAMES.

Do'-syo-wǎ. "*The place of basswoods.*" Name of Buffalo.

Gah-dah'-gĕh. "*Fishing-place with a scoop-basket.*" Cayuga Creek, or north fork of Buffalo Creek.

Hǎh-do'-neh. "*The place of June berries.*" Seneca Creek, or middle fork of Buffalo Creek.

Ga-e-nạ-dǎh'-daah. "*Slate rock bottom.*" Cazenovia Creek, or south fork of Buffalo Creek.

Tga-is'-da-ni-yọnt. "*The place of the suspended bell.*" The Seneca Mission House.

Tgah-sgoh'-sa-deh. "*The place of the falls.*" Falls above Jack Berry-town.

Jiihk'-do-waah'-gĕh. "*The place of the crab-apple.*" Cheektowaga.

De-as'-gwǎh-dǎ-ga'-neh. "*The place of the lamper-eel.*" Lancaster village, after a person of that name who resided there.

Ga-yǎh-gwǎǎh'-dọh. The Indian name of *Old Smoke*, who lived and died on the bank of Smoke's Creek. He led the Senecas at Wyoming. The name is now also applied to Smoke's Creek, and signifies "*The smoke has disappeared.*"

De-dyo'-deh-neh'-sak-dọ. "*A gravel bend.*" Lake shore above Smoke's Creek.

Jọ-nya'-dih. "*The other side of the flats.*" Tifft's farm.

De-yeh'-ho-gǎ-da-ses. "*The oblique ford.*" The old ford at the present Iron Bridge.

De-yoh'-ho-gǎh. "*The forks of the river.*" Junction of the Cayuga and Cazenovia creeks.

Tga'-nǫn-da-ga'-yos-hǎh. "*The old village.*" The flats embracing Twitchell's farm. This is the site of the first village the Senecas built on Buffalo Creek.

Ni-dyiǫ'-nyah-a'-ah. "*Narrow point.*" Farmer's Brothers Point.

Ga-nǫh'-hoh-gĕh. "*The place filled up.*" Long Point in Canada, and sometimes applied to Erie. In allusion to the Indian tradition, that The Great Beaver built a dam across Lake Erie, of which Presque Isle and Long Point are the remains.

Gah-gwah-ge'-gǎ-ạạh. "*The residence of the Kah-kwas.*" Eighteen Mile Creek. Sometimes called Gah-gwah'-gĕh.

Yǫ-da'-nyuh-gwah'. "*A fishing-place with hook and line.*" Sandytown, the old name for the beach above Black Rock.

Tgah'-si-yǎ-deh. "*Rope ferry.*" Old ferry over Buffalo Creek.

Tga-nǫh'-so-dǫh. "*The place of houses.*" Old village in the forks of Smoke's Creek.

Dyo-ge'-oh-ja-eh. "*Wet grass.*" Red Bridge.

Dyos'-hoh. "*The sulphur spring.*" Sulphur Springs.

De-dyo'-nạ-wạ'-ǫh. "*The ripple.*" Middle Ebenezer village.

Dyo-nǎh'-da-eeh. "*Hemlock elevation.*" Upper Ebenezer village, formerly Jack Berrytown.

Tgǎ-des'. "*Long prairie.*" Meadows above Upper Ebenezer.

O-nǫn'-dah-ge'-gah-gĕh. "*The place of the Onondagas.*" West end of Lower Ebenezer.

Sha-ga-nǎh'-gah-gĕh. "*The place of the Stockbridges.*" East end of Lower Ebenezer.

He-yǫnt-gat-hwat'-hah. "*The picturesque location.*" Cazenovia Bluff, east of Lower Ebenezer.

Dyo-e'-oh-gwes. "*Tall grass (or flag) island.*" Rattlesnake Island.

Dyu'-ne-ga-nooh'. "*Cold water.*" Cold Spring.

Gǎh-dǎ'-ya-deh. "*A place of misery.*" Williamsville. In allusion to the open meadows at this place, which were very bleak in winter. *Blacksmith* says the name refers to the "open sky," where the path crossed the creek.

www.ingramcontent.com/pod-product-compliance
Lightning Source LLC
Chambersburg PA
CBHW021436090426
42739CB00009B/1510